VAL'S BRIDGE

Published by Hansib Publications in 2012
London & Hertfordshire

Hansib Publications Limited
PO Box 226, Hertford, Hertfordshire, SG14 3WY
United Kingdom

Email: info@hansib-books.com
Web: www.hansib-books.com

A catalogue record of this book is available from the British Library

ISBN 978-1-906190-50-7

Printed and bound in the United Kingdom

VAL'S BRIDGE

by

Valerie Veronica Wood

VALERIE WOOD

Valerie, born in January 1960, was educated at Ducie High School, now Manchester Academy, where she had her first taste of leadership in her capacity as Head Girl. Leaving school, she spent the first nine years of her career in the Women's Royal Air Force (WRAF) progressing from Ground Stewardess to Air Stewardess, managing a middle team. During her time with the WRAF, she had the honour of meeting and serving members of the Royal Family.

Valerie has a long and distinguished career that took her all over the world. She was a Cabin Stewardess on the Queen Elizabeth II and Stewardess on the Royal Caribbean Cruise Lines, working on cruises between New York and the Caribbean. After a brief period as NVQ Co-ordinator, Valerie undertook administrative and Passenger Service roles with Servisair at Manchester Airport before joining British Airways.

Valerie is single and lives in Manchester.

PREFACE

Life is the quintessential journey whose navigation moulds the traveller. It is the people that you meet along the way who become your role models; the incentives you embrace to live out childhood dreams and the achievements and accomplishments that determine how successful that journey is. As you progress through life, there are numerous moments of indecision such as hearing but not heeding the words *'not ready for promotion'* for they encourage self-doubt and introduce a fear of failure.

I did not accomplish and achieve my goals in the sequence I desired; nonetheless it worked out better in my career. The enormity of challenges faced meant having to confront my self-doubt. Rejection and despondency will stall that smooth journey for you but in the face of adversity, the song says "don't stop believing, hold onto to that feeling". Feeling empowered to press on with your goals in life so you are not lost to history and playing your part in fulfilling your role and expanding one's sense of understanding.

I knew from an early age that I would write this book to inspire others. I was blessed with being brought up in a stable and loving home by my mother and father, until my father's sudden death. Thank God my mother's faith embolden her with a clarity of vision and a focused determination to take on the mantle of both father and mother, not remarry and instead concentrate on rearing and nurturing my sister and myself to make us be proud of the people we are today – to be the best person in your chosen career who happens to be black.

Ignorance and arrogance can lead to the fuelling of oppression. You may be the minority race but equally a minority achiever.

ACKNOWLEDGEMENTS

I wish to thank Arif Ali of Hansib Publications Limited. Belinda who spent many hours typing my manuscript. Jo, my English Language and Literature teacher, who became my role model. Janet who knew I had a story to tell. Whit Stennett, former Worshipful Mayor of Trafford and now Councillor, who gave me sound advice and support. Peter Kalu, Artistic Director of Commonword, who gave me the impetus and encouragement to expand my work.

I would also like to thank a number of people who know who they are.

VAL'S BRIDGE

CHAPTER ONE

MY EARLIEST CHILDHOOD

Through my parents and sister's eyes and memory, my life's journey began at the tender age of seven months old. Of course I do not have any personal memories at such a tender age but my parents' account of my birth is my starting point of this journey.

My mother was relieved when I finally arrived, unscathed, after nine months and 10 days in her womb because she had fallen over at eight months in sub zero temperatures, carrying a container of paraffin.

I was told that I was a quiet baby who did not make a fuss. Yet, at six months old I refused the breast and at seven months old I would climb out of my cot and stoke the open fire with my PJs. I loved music as a baby and would often stand in my cot holding on with one hand on the wooden rail and danced to Lady with the Red Dress on, and on, and on...!

My mother bought me a pair of red shoes when I was seven months old that I took my first steps in and walked for the first time. Those shoes remained on my feet whether I was asleep or awake. Those shoes were certainly made for walking as I would be through our front door at any given chance. I took that chance at 18 months old. In the open, I enjoyed the freedom of adventure, the smoke bellowing and belching out of chimneys and factories, the bell ringing on the red double-decker buses, a few cars beeping their horns....Then a family friend, Mr Alexander, spotted me and called out my name, Valerie! I stopped in my tracks.

During the 1950's Britain opened its doors to workers from its former colonies. My father took the opportunity and arrived in June 1956 persuaded by a dear family friend called Mr Reynold who served in the Royal Air Force (RAF) during the war. At the end of the war, Mr Reynold was rewarded for his services to the Mother Country and settled in England. He became a bus driver and invested his money into properties and pubs becoming one of the first black entrepreneurs.

An adult was always addressed as Mr or Miss as the use of first names was considered to be disrespectful. So Mr Alexander and Mr Reynold were just that – Mr.

My mother followed my father to the United Kingdom in September 1956 and soon found herself pregnant with my sister, Janet. They only intended to stay for five years but like so many other Caribbean people who migrated to the UK that return was consistently put back each year, resulting in 'permanent' residencies of 50 years and more. Yet the desire to return, whether in retirement or in death, never left them.

Moss Side, Manchester at the turn of the 19th century was a white middle class paradise. Sir Charles Hallé, pianist and conductor of the Hallé orchestra lived in the vicinity, there is a blue plaque commemorating his life between 1858 to 1895. However, all that changed with the settlement of Caribbean migrants who were actively recruited and encouraged to migrate to the UK to work in the country's national industries – Health and Transport especially. With each successive influx of new migrants to the country's major cities there was a consequent flight from them. In Moss Side, significant numbers of white residents chose to move out as Caribbean families moved in.

The Wood family moved in.

My late father, Kenneth, Janet and me at our eldest brother's Bertie wedding in July 1964

Mother Mary setting off to the local Seventh Day Adventist Church

Janet's graduation at Salford University as a BA Social Worker

Janet's wedding October 1990 with Bertie, Woody and Cecil flanking his sisters

Yvette's graduation at Georgetown Law School, Washington, DC, as a Doctor of Law

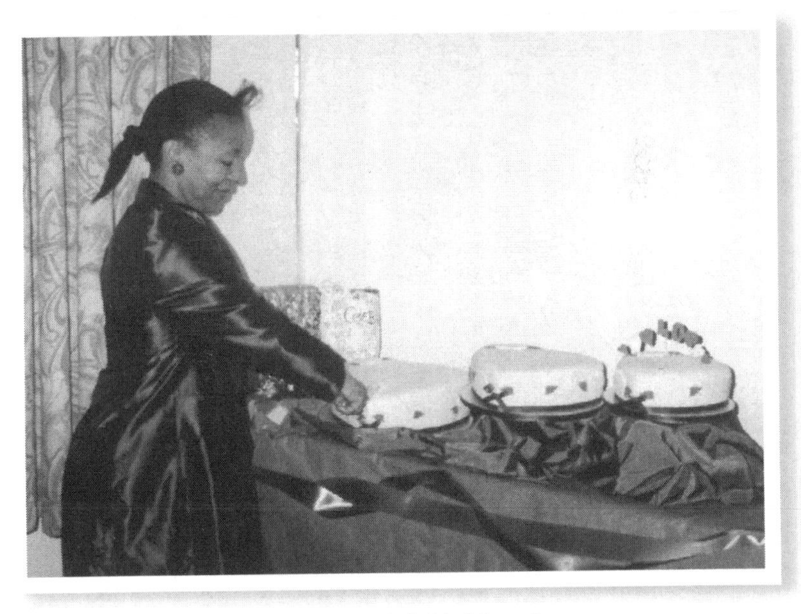

Cutting my Fortieth Birthday cake

Chelsea Pensioner friends

CHAPTER TWO

1960 – 1970

My father bought his own Victorian three-storey house for a mere £300 in 1960, six months after I was born. The house consisted of one living room, one dining room, five bedrooms, two kitchens and one bathroom. There were three other families living in the same dwelling – Mr Peregrine and Miss Naomi lived in the attic; Mr Leopold, Miss Ena and baby Ellis lived on the first floor back room and Patrick, Priscilla, Betty and Balfour in the front room on the first floor.

I had a happy and stable upbringing at Lloyd Street. My mother worked as a local Child Minder. Her duties as a Child Minder started at 4:30am and didn't finish until the last child left at 8pm. She worked as Child Minder and Mother seven days a week as she would be up early on a Saturday morning to wash and dress us for church. When we got back after the service we would have some lunch and then our Mum accompanied us, and other children in the area, to Stretford Road library to return our books and select new ones. It was important to my mother that we knew our 3R's.

Lloyd Street reminds me of the curry mile in Rusholme that comes to life in the evenings. During the summers in the 1960's and 1970's I remembered Lloyd Street bristling with a spate of activities – West Indian weddings, birthday parties or christenings. The DJ sounds would be booming and reverberating Ska, Rock Steady, Soca, Calypso and Reggae. From each end of Lloyd Street parties were held. If I had a restless night I would stand at the window and watch the night revellers returning home swinging and swaying from side to side.

But it is the weddings that held the most memorable recollections for me. Whilst no two weddings are the same, there are many common features and characteristics that are distinctive of a West Indian wedding. One actual wedding to remember was that of Charlene.

Charlene's wedding was not word-of-mouth. A proper invitation was sent and received because my sister Janet was a bridesmaid. Saturday 20 August 1969 was very hot and sunny with a temperature of 85°F. The sun was blazing down on my head; I felt it was on fire. I felt this searing heat penetrating my head, my skin was aglow with the soft sunrays with a bead of sweat across my forehead that sparkled like small gems held up to the light. My mother dressed me in a navy and white polka dot suit and the coat was the reverse; white tights, white shoes and a navy handbag. Sarah my close friend was also dressed identical.

In the rush to be ready for the wedding the family of the bride forgot to pick up my sister who was fortuitously and frantically transported by a family friend.

When asked to be a bridesmaid, parents of the bride, by tradition, provided the dress, headgear and shoes for all the bridesmaids. There was no dress rehearsal. My sister arrived at the church on time but nervous and shy at meeting the other bridesmaids; her palms were sweaty with anxiety. Janet soon realised, to her consternation, that she was one in a procession of 12 bridesmaids grouped in three different colours! The bride's mother, Kathleen, told my mother that Janet would be wearing lime-green. To Janet's surprise, she was in a different shade of lime green and style to the bridesmaids who were supposed to be in her colour.

The Chief Bridesmaid, a coveted position, wore a full-length orange dress with miniscule orange pearls running down the centre of the back, orange skullcap with a white feather protruding on the left side, white gloves and white-heeled sling back shoes.

The Maid of Honour, similarly coveted, wore a powder blue long puff sleeve dress. The front of the dress had a plunging neckline and was set off with a powder blue skullcap, white pearl earrings and matching necklace and white court shoes.

There were also a group of three bridesmaids in different shades of pink – the first of the group wore a powder pink full-length dress with a floppy collar, a pink carnation clipped on the left side of her head and white leather pumps; the second bridesmaid wore a fuchsia mid-calf dress with a round collar, a fuchsia headband and white sling back shoes. The third bridesmaid wore a pink skullcap, matching pink pearl earrings and necklace, a high necked full-length pink long sleeved dress and white flat heeled-shoes.

The second group of three bridesmaids were dressed in yellow and were very similar in pale chiffon mid-length dresses that had a round collar and a belt, short sleeve with white gloves and two-inch heeled court shoes. They wore a crown of lilies in their hair.

It seemed like a carnival masquerade party instead of a wedding where the tradition is white and subtle colours but this was wedding Caribbean style!

The guests were filing into the church pews at incredible speed so as not to miss the "spectacle" that was being played out in front of their eyes. Like every other wedding – Caribbean or British – there was an air of heightened expectation that preceded the arrival of the bride. This was further enhanced when word got around that 400 guests were invited to this wedding which made it the biggest wedding in Moss Side for many years. Women in their best church outfit or a new sale outfit; Men in their black/brown double-breasted pin striped suits with their watch dangling from the pockets on a chain, two-tone leather shoes or a blazer with chinos and open necked shirts and Panama hats assuming they were going punting dominated the scene.

The children of these gaggling adults looking wide-eyed and bushy tailed at the excitement that surrounded them. One little girl caught my eye in her red satin knee-length dress with matching hair ribbons and handbag that had a silver butterfly badge pinned to it. Her red shoes reminded me of my first shoes that my mother bought me at seven months old. She sat next to her mother sedately watching with keen bright eyes and great anticipation of this spectacle that was unfolding before her.

I imagined if I was getting married how would I feel on my big day, as every little girl's wish is to get married to her suitor in 'shining armour'. My head started whirling with the count of bridesmaids and pageboys. My eyes started spinning in my head with the cost of my wedding. I felt nauseated with the smell of cheap perfume wafting up my nostrils. My hands were moist with anticipation of the bride's arrival.

Janet and two bridesmaids were dressed in different shades of lime green satin – a lined full-length dress with satin skullcaps, white gloves and white sling-back heels.

There were two flower girls with pink-laced stick out dresses, pink headbands, white gloves and white pumps and last, but not least, one pageboy in a black suit, nylon socks and black patent buckled shoes.

The clicking of heels spelt the arrival of Derek, the bridegroom. His skin was fresh decked out in his fine black suit, white frilled shirt, black pointed shoes and thick black bow tie; the essence of sartorial excellence Caribbean style. His hair was shiny and wavy with Brylcream. He also had a white handkerchief in his breast pocket.

The bride, Charlene, arrived in her full regalia – tiara that glistened in the baking sun with its 'crown jewels' and a lace veil that had a 12 foot trail with every foot of the trail decorated with a cluster of five crystals. The high necked dress with its puffed sleeves tapered at the cuffs had a high waist that swirled around with crystals. The bottom half of the dress was straight with a background of satin matching the shoes that Charlene wore. Her feet moved gently down the aisle to The Bridal March by Wagner.

Her stepfather, Brian, looked into his daughter's eyes brimming with pride. Charlene was six years old when they met and he raised her as his own. The local vicar of Christ Church on Monton Street conducted the service which included the wedding vows to honour and obey. The bride and groom were given permission to kiss and the bridal procession then sauntered down the aisle and stopped at the top of the Church stairs to be showered in confetti and also for the photographer with his sixties Olympus camera to snap a handful of pictures for the album.

The bride and groom were driven to the reception venue – a local hall – in a borrowed Humber, decorated with neutral colour ribbons.

The hall with its unexpected cleanliness was graced with a horseshoe table covered with white paper tablecloth. The sombre wooden tables by the walls were left undressed and were occupied by the overspill of the congregation. The tables vibrated from the music blaring out and the drinkers plonking their liquor glasses on them reminiscent of the flourish with which dominoes are placed on the playing surface.

The live naked wires from the speakers meant *'do not touch'* for fear any mishaps could spoil the entire wedding reception which had great expectations of finishing at 5am. The DJ sounds booming and echoing Ska, Rock Steady, Calypso, Soca and Reggae. It was a sultry atmosphere with plumes of smoke twirling in mid-air from the Havana cigars and Woodbine cigarettes.

The gaiety of the children playing 'a ring a ring of roses' until they all toppled over each other, until you heard less and less of them as fatigue settled in and one child could be found huddled in a ball under a table, another sprawled out on a chair and so on. Their parents immediately notified by the wedding party to take their child/children home.

I hid my small frame behind an artificial wall as I was not ready to leave just yet. The party had just got started and I was having a good time!

My mother who is a Christian wanted to go home. My sister wanted to go home also. My father was staying a while longer and I wanted to stay and dance the night away whether my father was staying or not. My mother left with Janet at around 11pm and my father was instructed to keep an eye on me and not to stay too long by my mother. My father did not like weddings but succumbed to this one because my sister was a participant.

My father tried to take me home at 12 midnight but failed. He tried again at 1am, 2am and I finally gave in at around 2:30am with fatigue. My father had to carry me home and was not happy, as I was nine at the time. My mother was not happy as she had been waiting up thinking that he would be home with me at the latest 12 midnight. She changed my clothes and put me to bed and I could hear her rebuking me through my drowsiness. Janet was fast asleep sprawled over the double bed which we shared. She became miserable when my mother tried to move her to the next side of the bed.

I started nursery on my fourth birthday and soon settled into play acting in the mornings being teacher, pastor or ballerina and then a siesta in the afternoon. I would continue my roles at home that I had acted out that day.

As a childminder, my mother cared for up to 12 children between the ages of four to nine. I would often assist my mother by keeping the children occupied at certain times during the day until their parents picked them up after work. The status of women in the 60's/70's was as the homemaker whilst the husband, if he was present, provided everything for the family. There were some single women who, out of necessity, had to leave their child/children attended or unattended and go to work to provide for them.

One evening I was playing the role of a pastor and was about to baptise Marjorie who was a slim girl. My mother caught me in the act and the basin full of cold water gushed everywhere and I rushed up the stairs as fast as I could, aware that I was in deep trouble!

Every August Bank Holiday my mother took me and the children who lived in the vicinity that she cared for to Belle Vue Zoo and Funfair. It was a great day out as it broke up the mundane six weeks school holidays. All the children were walking and talking as we crossed a small bridge that was constructed over the lion's den. My mother accounted for everyone walking over the bridge safely except for Raymond who was pre-occupied watching a lion, watching him who was very hungry! My mother shouted at Raymond so vociferously that he picked up his feet and ran to catch up with the rest of us.

One sunny Sunday afternoon I was playing on the pavement outside my home with some neighbourhood friends when two sisters and their brother, who lived on the other side of the street, called us some nasty words. I was shocked, did my Highway code, crossed the road into no–man's land and poked my stubby index finger into the face of the oldest sibling for not setting an example to her younger sister and brother. Her mother heard her daughter screaming and came out of her house to ascertain what had happened. I fled across the road and back to safety and punched the air in victory! The mother stood with her hands akimbo.

The children that my mother cared for are now adults and have studied and embarked in different careers in Sales, the Probation Service, Social Care and Investment Banking. They now have children and grand children of their own and have instilled in them the values that my mother first taught them.

I needed a new adventure to take me away from the humdrum of home life and found it when I got the travel bug during the mid-sixties. My mother and I would leave Janet at home and travel to Ringway airport (now Manchester) on a red double-decker bus. It was breathtaking scenery. The vista, the verge around the buildings I passed on the bus on my journey. I was in awe of the airport and its impressive buildings. We would sit on the open terrace and have our lunch while the planes took off and landed in front of our eyes. It was both exciting and exhilarating.

My eyes were full of glee as an aircraft taxied to the runway as it lined up and sauntered into the air. I would spend endless hours mesmerised as airlines were given permission to take off and land by air traffic control. I knew then, this was my future destiny. I felt the 'shackles' of the family expectation that I would become a teacher unleashed. My family history has centred on academia and I felt the pull to remain in this arena. But here I was being drawn to the passion of flying and I felt that I had the guts to hold on to that passion.

On my way home I would relive the day's events and come to a satisfactory conclusion on how I would operate a flight. During my lunch breaks at school I would look up to the piercing blue sky and see an aircraft soaring high above my head and would cease playing in pure wonderment of the aerodynamics of flight. I felt ethereal about living amongst the nimbus and cumulus clouds. At my local newsagent I would look for magazines on aviation; this would pre-occupy me especially during the harsh winter months of the 1960's.

My earliest responsibility came at the age of nine when I became the school monitor at Webster Junior School. Half an hour before lunchtime I and the other school monitors would prepare for lunch in the school canteen. After lunch, if the duty teacher was not available in the school playground I felt I was in charge! It was unique for the school's playground to be built on top of the roof of the building. The school was built nearly one hundred years earlier. The building seemed so empty and vacuous with its sash windows that required a long pole to open and close them. The high aertex ceilings and stone walls felt like a sanatorium. When the bell rang for afternoon lessons I would line up the children by year and march them to their classroom. Mr Thurrow, the Headmaster and Mr Williams, his Deputy were silently amused when they heard that I decided the children were my 'responsibility'.

CHAPTER THREE

1970 – 1980

In the early 70's I joined the Pathfinder Group at my local branch of the Seventh-day Adventist church. This enabled me to join in with different activities such as sewing, cooking, baking, orienteering (ordinance survey map and compass), first aid, Highway Code, mountaineering (Mount Snowdon) and swimming. This opportunity also allowed me to playact my favourite role as hostess.

We would meet every Sunday morning between the hours of 10 o'clock to three o'clock, to sell magazines in the suburbs of Manchester and to raise funds for our annual Whitsun camp week. The money raised would help to subsidise my fee; it was a week of outdoor pursuits where, at times, I was selected as team leader.

On Monday 22nd March 1971 my mother had heard the news that a family friend had died, her reply was "who is next?" There is a belief among Caribbean people that bad news comes in threes. Little did I realise that there may be some truth in this.

In the early hours of Thursday morning my world was turned upside down when my father suffered a fatal paralytic stroke and brain haemorrhage. Brain haemorrhages are common on my father's side of the family; both his father and grandfather succumbed to it. He was an only child and his wish was to be sent back to Jamaica to be buried next to his parents. This wish my mother granted and sent my eldest brother, Bertie, as a sign of respect and to represent the family in England.

In retrospect my mother felt that all the family should have travelled to Jamaica but she was not thinking straight.

My father's body was viewed at Leech's Funeral Parlour by hundreds of people spilling out onto the kerb who were from the community; my father's body lying in a wooden inner face and a zinc outer face coffin that was deliberately chosen to seal the body for its journey to Jamaica via London. I was not ready to look at my father for the last time so I stayed with a neighbour. The coffin was too heavy for the weight and balance of the aircraft so the decision was taken by the undertakers that it would travel by road to London and then transported by air to Jamaica.

His body was received by his favourite first cousin, Miss Mae, who later reported to my mother that the funeral arrangements went like clockwork. Miss Mae was a retired Headmistress and Magistrate who I saw once as a child at a family wedding in London in the mid-sixties.

In later years when I visited my father's tomb, I found his final resting place is on a beautiful hilltop overlooking the village of Facey, Troja, St. Catherine where he was born. This land was bequeathed to Bertie, my eldest brother, by our paternal grandparents as he was the first grandchild.

As a child of 11 years of age I went into a trance mode and felt numb. Janet had a partial breakdown when our father suddenly passed away. I found out many years later after I finally went for bereavement counselling, encouraged by Janet, that the signs and symptoms we experienced are normal for children to experience whilst adults find it more difficult to come to terms with a loss. My mother took on the mantle of father and mother and had no desire to remarry. **I did not know my father on a personal level** but remember playacting with him. I would make afternoon tea and we would go to the local park and sit under the figurine of Edward VII and have sandwiches and cakes from the picnic basket that I had packed and carried with my friend Sharon. This he found very amusing and would relay the story to my mother of the picnic event.

My father was a burly man of six feet four inches who had piercing blue eyes, a white complexion and grey-haired. My father was 54 and a middle-aged man when I was born. My maternal great-grandfather left Scotland in the early 1850's and boarded a ship bound for Jamaica. Legend has it that Robbie Burns was also a passenger on that ship but was struck down with an undiagnosed illness and was offloaded. The story behind my great-grandfather's migration goes back to 1746 when the Mc Farlanes who sided with Bonnie Prince Charlie were defeated at the battle of Culloden. The clan was disbanded and were forced to join the McPherson clan. They too were persecuted and moved from the highlands to the lowlands. My great-grandfather decided to take his wealth and set sail for Jamaica.

My great-grandfather Andrew McGraw settled in the parish of St Catherine, very fertile land for arable farming. He married a local woman called Louise and had my grandmother Alice Maude around 1876 whom my father is the spitting image of from the stories I have been told even though I have never seen her portrait. I hope that one day I will be able to fit the last piece of the jigsaw puzzle in discovering why my great-grandfather chose to emigrate to Jamaica instead of one of the other commonwealth countries such as Canada, Australia or New Zealand.

I joined my sister, Janet, at our local high school, Ducie Technical, in 1971. Former girls used to wear boaters and ankle socks with their shoes. As part of my uniform I wore a beret and knee length socks. The school became a comprehensive between 1971 and 1973 and converted back to a technical school in 1974 giving girls the opportunity to learn woodwork, engineering, drawing, etc. In 2002 it became Manchester Academy which is privately funded.

I adjusted to high school very easily. The school was racially mixed with students of various cultural backgrounds. My schoolhouse was Worsley and I was very proud to represent the house. In my third year I was selected as Prefect and subsequently became Head Girl in 1977. This was my first taste of leadership, sitting-in on staff meetings, discussing with the staff concerns that pupils had raised, taking the Sixth Form assembly with the Head Boy, Roland Peters. My English and Literature teacher, Miss Brambles, for whom I still have the greatest of reverence for noticed the impish devil in me but knew I had the potential to achieve and accomplish my future goals.

Before I knew it seven years had passed at school and I was about to embark on my future career. I left school with a handful of 'O' levels. A large percentage of the pupils felt the school had academically underachieved because we languished in the middle of the school league table exam results.

In the 70's as a teenager I welcomed the freedom of visiting other parts of the city of Manchester, as my mother was a strict character this was not easy. She would allow me to visit a gospel church group fronted by a lady called Mrs Nembitt. Mrs Nembitt would converse with my mother about church outings, this was pleasing to my mother's ear and this was my freedom to travel around the city and to other parts of the country. Youth clubs was only something I could dream of as it was off limits.

On a Saturday wintry evening Mrs Nembitt arranged with my mother that she and Mr Nembitt would pick me up at

17:00 to travel to Huddersfield for a Youth Convention with the rest of the gospel group. My friend Angela who never misses a trip could not make this one because her mother was not well. I spent two hours pampering myself and finally dressed in my sister's leopard coat and hat and my leather brown laced-up knee length boots feeling like the 'Queen of Sheba'.

I noticed the time was ticking away and Mr and Mrs Nembitt had still not arrived. It was 18:00 and with no telephone number to call I just had to wait. They finally arrived at 18:30. The reason they were late was the van had an alternator problem and they still had to pick up the nine people who were also travelling to Huddersfield.

The concert was due to start at 20:00 so we would arrive in sufficient time. As we left the sign of Manchester behind us, the van became problematic and conducted a merry dance chugging along, stopping abruptly, belching carbon monoxide and struggling on. This continued for another five minutes before the van completely shut down.

The nearest breakdown rescue telephone box was a short distance from where the van broke down. Mr Nembitt who was asthmatic became short of breath due to the chilly weather. Richard went to make a distress call from the telephone box to the AA who said they would be with us in two hours time! We decided the best way to keep ourselves busy was to sing gospel choruses to keep us warm and in high spirits. After an hour we noticed a coach passing that seemed full of Caribbean people dressed to the hilt going in the same direction that we wanted to travel. This deflated any high spirits that we had left; morale was also on the wane. We sat sedately in our own thoughts until the AA vehicle arrived on the scene.

He managed to fix the alternator which was 'the thorn in

our side'. We were shortly on our way – but not in the direction of Huddersfield. We collectively decided to return to Manchester as we had already missed the concert and the time was 23:00.

I arrived home at 23:45 cold, hungry and miserable.

In May 1975 as part of an English Literature group trip it was proposed by Miss Brambles to take us to Scotland to visit the area of Glencoe where the Mc Donalds and the Campbells fought over land supremacy. This is the region where "Ring of Bright Waters" was written by Robin Maxwell that we were studying as one of the set texts. It was a lifetime adventure. It was the year preceding the heat wave of 1976. We were loaned the school's Variety Club award 12-seater bus that was presented to the school by Farouk Engineer, the Indian cricketer who played for Lancashire Cricket Club as wicket keeper. Mr Shrivers was the driver who doubled up as the Physics teacher, Miss Brambles and the pupils were: Hazel, Jane, Sheila, Abigail, Lydia, Karen and myself. It was a week of sailing, yachting, canoeing, fishing, pony-trekking, orienteering, mountaineering (Ben Nevis) and camping.

We drove up through Stirling University where Miss Brambles' sister was studying History and Law. We enjoyed a tea break and travelled onto Fort William where there was a tug boat waiting to take us to our retreat at Mallaig, Inverness. The girls would take it in turn each evening to row out into Loch Lommond and cast the net with an instructor.

Each morning the net was hauled in by one of us. Salmon was always the catch which we had for dinner for the week. During the week's activities my notoriety soon grew when on a gentle short walk between two ridges near the retreat my expertise in navigation was amiss in attempting to take two of the girls across a stream that lay below a plunging rock face.

The day was fine with a blue sky and puffs of cloud; the moss and heather along the roadside had grown tired and weary from the heat we were experiencing. Hazel, Sheila and myself were hurrying back to our lodge for some dinner and I volunteered to put my orienteering skills to good use.

The ground below my feet was firm, hard and level as I proceeded across a rippling stream. Between a wall and some shrubbery there was a rope of smooth wire and I felt we could cross the stream. As I put my left foot forward the earth underneath my foot gave way and I stumbled back onto my haunches. I remembered the saying 'long road brings sweat, short road brings blood'. My second escapade came when the pony instructor (who was the nephew of General Montgomery) asked me if I had heard his instructions when leaving the stables which I timidly replied yes. As I was leaving the stables I failed to notice a thin wire above the gate which nearly throttled me, luckily my high necked red thick woollen jumper saved me from sustaining a severe injury to my neck.

The instructor was not amused. Further instructions were given not to shout as we were on a narrow ridge because the ponies would be alarmed and could bolt. Abigail's pony Prince came up on my inside and startled my pony over the edge. I shouted and my pony sped off just like in the 'Bonanza TV Series'. My pony narrowly missed putting its head through a rusty wire.

The third and final part to this story was not to allow the ponies to lower their heads to drink from the stream we were crossing as the rest of the ponies would bunch up behind. My strength to my pony was zilch; the instructor came charging over and ordered me off my pony and told me I was a 'dangerous woman' and told to walk the mile back to the retreat. I was terribly upset and was inconsolable.

The next stage of my career was when I took my attestation on 23 October 1978 in the Royal Air Force career's office which was located on Market Street, Manchester. There was a short ceremony where I pledged my allegiance to the Queen along with four other girls who would travel to Hereford with me on 24th October. There were about 60 girls who had travelled from all over the UK and Northern Ireland. Some looked shocked – a sense of being overwhelmed.

"What am I doing here?" Some initial feelings of self-doubt as the reality of change became apparent. But that soon dissipated as integration increases self-esteem.

We were waiting for the Corporal drill instructors who arrived at the stipulated time written on our briefs. Some girls had recently taken a holiday and were fresh and suntanned and dressed in gaudy and outlandish coloured tops and skirts whilst others were dressed in sombre suit pants. All the girls had one or two bags; I had six suitcases. My mother and sister decided to pack all and sundry for me as if I was a prima donna. I struggled and had to make two to three trips to retrieve my luggage on the journey from the station to the camp.

The five stages of group development occurred with the forming of groups, nervousness and polite conversation, personalities starting to emerge as girls vied for positions. Then these group settling and personalities strengthened with some banter and joking and finally, groups pulling together and leaving a legacy of camaraderie.

I joined the Women's Royal Air Force at the age of 18 years six months and went to RAF Hereford for an intensive six-week training, enjoyable but equally gruelling. I would be up at 5:30am Monday to Friday with marching sessions commencing at 6:30am and a break at seven for breakfast. Then, General knowledge of the Royal Air Force, Ground Defence Training, First Aid, PE, Maths and English. Lunch and dinner would be fitted in when it was convenient to eat. Training sessions would only finish upon completion.

There was the occasional outing to Winchester Cathedral and Worcester. Hereford is a sleepy market town that comes to life on a Saturday morning. I was grateful for lie-ins on Saturday mornings but would look forward to taking the bus to the centre of town which was a half an hour journey from the RAF campus.

The building I lived in for six weeks was called Nicholson – D block. There were four dormitories of 15 girls, a flight of 60. The building was built 100 years ago with its gargoyles (Medusa's relatives) protruding over the face of the block; the worn and chipped buttresses, the high ceilings and sash windows.

The Recruitment Leader's bed was closest to the door – that was mine. Each morning the reveille sounded at 05:30am and at six o'clock there was a bunk inspection which I had to pass. Bull-nights were twice a week. This was to ensure that the block remained clean at all times. We would take it in turns to clean the floor; I rolled up my sleeves and steered this bull machine with bristles from side to side making sure that I polished every square inch.

During those six weeks training I wrote home twice complaining of feeling homesick and was told by my mother and sister that I would get over it. Thankfully I did! During my fitness exercises I would run the 800m in two minutes and 10 seconds; over two minutes and 15 seconds would be a failure.

The gas chamber was part of the Ground Defence Training. I would be ordered to take off my gas mask and shout out my service number. These were the strenuous times that sapped at my inner strength. I have since pulled out my pictures from my album on my joining anniversary and wonder what is everyone doing with their lives, especially the seven girls who were medically discharged and the eight for lack of discipline. Also, the Corporal Drill Instructors, the Drill Sergeant, the Commissioned Officer in charge and who oversaw the training and Geraldine Bowen who won the Recruitment sash.

The build up to my passing out parade was very exciting but I wasn't sure if Janet would be there for my passing out ceremony. I waited patiently inside the red telephone kiosk for her call which I did not receive. My heart sunk in despair, my throat felt dry, my eyes moist with sadness. I slumped to the ground and started sobbing until my stomach ached in pain. The next morning I was pleasantly surprised to find she was in the crowd when I gave my "eyes right" for the salute from the Station Commander who was stood on the dais.

This picture was captured on film by a colleague's mother, as my sister had forgotten her camera. It was 6th December 1978 as I stood to attention for the Station Commander's inspection; it was bitterly cold with my left nostril dribbling. I completely ignored it. I was immaculately dressed in my No1's – fitted air force blue jacket matching below the knee skirt, pale blue starched shirt, black tie, natural coloured tights, highly polished laced up shoes and a forage hat.

After the ceremony I went up to my sister and gave her a big hug and thanked her for attending. My sister looked regal in an off white cashmere coat, matching pillbox hat, black leather gloves, boots and handbag. She apologised for missing my call and explained she was late home from work, hurriedly packed and went to sleep to wake early. There were refreshments laid on for our loved ones and ourselves where we could meet and reminisce with the staff.

Although I blended in with the girls I felt during my initial training they resented the fact that I held the position as a Recruitment Leader. The only colour I was interested in was blue. I felt there was a pang of jealousy and bigotry which was clearly detected from quite a wide range of sources throughout my career.

I went home for a well earned Christmas break and returned to Hereford in the New Year for my catering course in January 1979. I enquired about becoming a cabin crew member and was informed that I would need at least two years assessments on the ground to apply for cabin crew. I was taught at the prestigious Hereford Catering Squadron by a distinguished instructor and a great mentor called Timothy who had worked on Queen's flight at RAF Benson and also RAF Northolt and taught me silver service, bar reception, reception and valeting. He exquisitely showed me how to peel an orange for royalty; this put me in good stead for my royal duties that followed shortly.

My catering instructor knew that I had opted for RAF Brize Norton as my first choice camp (home of the Vicker's VC10) but I was disappointed when my second choice RAF High Wycombe, Strike Command headquarters became available. It was a busy place. The base accommodated a helicopter pad and occasionally a helicopter landed. I covered guard duties which were mandatory during my tour at the base. The Guardroom was located inside the main gates of the camp. My duty commenced at 06:00am until 18:00pm with a tea and lunch break. My sentry duties were carried out in a port-a-cabin fitted with a heater, a kettle and TV. During the rush hours between 08:00 – 10:00 and 16:00 – 18:00 I was constantly saluting the commissioned badge on the officers' hats passing in and out of the gates. My wrist was wracked with pain. The excruciating pain travelled up my right arm until it reached my upper shoulder.

I was dressed in my No2 uniform and not my No1 as I did for my passing out parade. There were bus loads of airmen and women being ferried from the domestic camp (No3) to HQ (No1).Private vehicles stopping to show their permits. The Station Commander's car with the RAF ensign fluttering in the wind brought me to attention with a smart salute. The military buses that transported airmen and women to Head Quarters stopped inside the gates and dropped of their passengers who scattered like an army of ants to their places of work. They worked in Commcent (communications network where annual paper exercise are held), Human Resources, Telephone Exchange and the Command Medical and Dental Administration Offices. The highest base ranking officer was an Air Vice-Marshal and the lowest rank was a pilot officer; a squadron leader's rank was nicknamed a teaboy! War paper exercises were held annually.

The camp was nestled in the Chiltern Hills and the Navy Army Air Force Institution (NAAFI) in conjunction with the Chiltern 100 Club. RAF High Wycombe was a good place to learn my trade. I covered what I had learnt on my catering course and how to pack a piece of luggage for royalty and turn down a divan, etc.

I became the personal stewardess for the Counter Tactical Task Organisation officer who held the rank of Air Commodore. I would attend dinner parties on a weekend and heard conversations to which only I was privy to. In the officer's mess I would be assigned the top table for the function that would be held that particular day. This brought me in contact with 'Bomber Harris' who spearheaded many air raids over Germany during WWII and who was celebrating his 80th birthday.

I was also involved in arranging a Royal Pack, which consisted of china, glassware and cutlery which had the Queen's insignia stamped on it. The pack would be dispatched to Whitehall and other London landmarks for military events. I was also involved in setting up local packs for presentations and conferences at Strike Command. One particular day a black cab was booked to take me from the Officers mess (No2 camp) to Headquarters (No1 camp). As the taxi driver sped away and took a corner, the urn full of boiling hot water turned over in the back of the taxi cab. I managed to alleviate myself from the onrush of hot water and precariously holding the side of the urn saved some of the water for the coffee and tea break. The windows were foggy and inside was like a sauna. Fortunately all the officers had tea or coffee and were none the less wiser to what had occurred in the cab.

Stag dining in-nights were rowdy and raucous. The evening would begin very formal with a hammer and gavel on the top table where grace was given, a five course meal followed with gentlemen throwing rolls and food at each other. The evening would end with the aroma of cigars and liqueurs. My starched white jacket and gloves remained pristine.

In July 1979 the announcement that the Prince of Wales would be visiting brought the camp to life. Everyone from the Station Commander to the cleaner had a duty to perform. The second occasion that I performed royal duties for Prince Charles was at RAF Bentley Priory, Middlesex for the 40th anniversary of the Gloster Meteors. Unfortunately, Princess Diana could not attend the engagement as Prince William was teething. I was selected ahead of 25 others at Brize Norton for the Royal Engagement. On arrival at Bentley Priory I met with the other selected members of staff from bases within the region. With 48 hours before the big day there were candelabras, pepper and salt pots to silver polish; glassware, chinaware and cutlery with the Queen's insignia to prepare; the mahogany furniture and burgundy upholstery to be rearranged; napkins folded and counted, correct name cards, menu cards and place mats counted; flowers to be ordered and wine, whisky, sherry, port and an array of liqueurs delivered.

The chef ordered the food for the meal in advance including tea and coffee beverages. A rehearsal took place 24 hours prior to the visit with all the staff involved with the function.

On the day of the visit the dozen staff selected to serve were excited at the prospect of meeting His Royal Highness the Prince of Wales. I had met Charles previously but was eager to meet Her Royal Highness, who later became Diana the Princess of Wales and emerged as the People's Princess. Diana was also a Cancerian like my mother and sister and I knew how kind, generous and giving they are by nature.

At 12:00 the staff were stood down and instructed to return for 15:00. I showered and dressed immaculate with my hair swept back into a chignon. I wore natural makeup with a touch of red lipstick with my pristine white jacket and gloves and powder blue epaulettes worn for Royal functions; Air Force blue skirt, pale blue shirt, black tie, flesh coloured tights and highly polished black laced up shoes. I tried to remain cool, calm and collected on the outside but inside my stomach was churning over like butter.

At 15:30 the staff were given a final uniform and hygiene inspection. Guests started arriving at 15:45, the scent of expensive perfume and aftershave wafted around the anteroom where cocktails were served to the ladies and gentlemen. The men dressed in black tie and the ladies in knee length or full length dresses from the top haute couture designers with matching jewellery and coiffures. The hustle and bustle of the wine waiter's replenishing their trays with fresh glasses of cocktails as soon as they disappeared off the tray. Conversation amongst the guests became muted as the time was fast approaching for the arrival of HRH Prince of Wales.

At 16:00 Prince Charles arrived on his own, word spread like wildfire that Princess Diana would not be attending the engagement as Prince William was teething.

How bitterly disappointed I was that I was not meeting her. My eyes welled up and my throat became dry from the plumes of smoke swirling around in the room. It proved to be the only occasion I would have met the People's Princess. I dusted myself down in the mirror and told myself I have a duty to perform.

The RAF musicians who were positioned in the foyer struck up 'A Blaze Of Light' on their musical instruments as he entered the building. The customary meets and greets by the Station Commander, The Adjutant, Warrant Officer in charge of the officers Mess and Head Chef. He joined the guests designated to meet him in the anteroom waiting patiently to be introduced to him.

At 17:00 the Warrant officer spoke to Prince Charles aid that early dinner is served. When everyone was seated grace was given by the Master of Ceremonies and the RAF Latin motto *Per Ardua Ad Astra* (Through Adversity to the Stars) was said. I stood at my station as the commis and my veg commis, on the signal from the Warrant officer, cleared the starters that were pre-laid on each table. The entrée, main course and dessert were all served from the left and cleared in from the right.

The main course was served out of a terrine precariously sat on a damp serving cloth and also the vegetables. Upon the signal from the Flight Sergeant (the W.O.'s deputy) the wine waiter's served white wine from the right of the guest with their starter and red wine with the entrée thereafter with not a drop spilt onto the well polished grained table.

The RAF band played A Blaze Of Light, Winds, Skywriter, Skywatch, Cavalry Of The Clouds, Out Of The Blue and Strike up the Band during the five course meal consisting of: a starter, entrée, main course, sorbet and dessert. After the meal was served the guests were served tea or coffee from the right and offered a cigar or cigarette out of the box from the left. Liquers were also served to the guests, whilst others decided to have a liqueur when they retired to the anteroom. It is protocol that no one leaves the party before a member of the Royal Family.

Another memorable event centred around my sporting life. As a student, I was selected to play netball and badminton for Ducie High and netball for Manchester. Netball is a very physical game for young ladies to play. It's fierce, ferocious, invigorating and exhilarating.

I went on to represent the WRAF in netball and WRAFG in badminton. Matches were held after office hours but a tournament meant the team were exempt from duties because we were representing the WRAF. One game that had all these attributes was a tournament game against RAF Upavon for the Group Winners Trophy. The girls for the Brize Norton including myself arrived at the gym for the one and a half hour journey to Upavon. Everyone was pent up as this trophy meant a lot to us as players representing the station.

We were the crème de la crème who had fought off other girls to be selected as Goalkeeper, Goal shooter, Goal attack,

Wing attack, Centre (myself and captain), Wing defence and Wing attack. The journey which was normally filled with the girls catching up on gossip, bursting with laughter and cackling like geese was instead sombre as if there was a funeral to attend. Someone broke the gloom hanging in the air and tried to gee everyone up with the up-coming Royal wedding, but there was only a murmur emanating from their lips in a sign of polite acknowledgement. The journey seemed endless. I noticed some of the girls hands were clasped in 'prayer' – everyone in their own thoughts as to how we were going to beat the team that seemed invincible and who had won all the accolades that they competed for in netball. Abruptly we arrived when someone announced 'welcome to Upavon'.

We gathered our minds and thoughts and with our possessions headed for the gym. We had half an hour practice before the game commenced. We huddled in a circle, said a word of prayer and placed our right hands in the circle on top of each other in a sign of unity. We were going to need effective communication, be outstanding on the court and an element of luck. Mrs Wiley our Physical Education instructor gave us one last piece of advice during warm up and that was to stick to our markers and to be proud of ourselves for reaching this far in the tournament. Reaching this far, all we wanted to do was WIN!

Upavon won the toss and chose to keep the ball. The whistle blew and battle commenced. The opponents kept the ball for the first ten minutes of the game teasing and tantalising us as if we were food on the end of a spoon. They were trying to get my team out of position but we stuck to our markers like glue. The game is played in two halves of 30 minutes. We felt, as a team, they were in possession of the ball for too long and in command of the game. We took matters into our own hands and the Brize

Norton wing attack managed to prize the ball out of the goalkeeper's hand.

Wing attack shouted: 'it's my ball'.

Goal attack yelled: 'pass to me so I can shoot'

The ball was lofted into the net.

We built up a commanding lead at the end of the first 30 minutes – Brize Norton 10, Upavon 4. We knew we could not sit back on our laurels. We would continue to remain in possession and build on our lead. During the ten minutes interval our confidence soared to tumultuous heights, our instructor advised us to go and win it.

The second half started. Concentrate, I kept saying to myself. My heart was pounding against my vest; I kept regurgitating my saliva. My head pounding with the chanting coming from the few supporters that travelled with us. The smell of the rubber ball exchanging sweaty palms shot up spurts of evaporation. I lunged at my opposite centre to retrieve the ball and sent her crashing to the floor. The referee blew on her whistle to stop play. I was deemed to have fouled her still lying prostrate on the floor. She gathered her crumpled body up and got to her feet. She threw the ball to her wing attack, wing attack threw to the goal shooter and she netted the ball.

The score was now 10 v 8. I was swept with fear, we can't lose now. The last five minutes of the game were hellish as both teams strived to play at a ferocious speed, moving gracefully across the court with the ball in hand.

Finally the whistle blew and my legs buckled under my body frame. 10 v 8! We won. I was elated but equally exhausted. After receiving my individual medal I held the trophy aloft towards our supporters who had cheered us on and to say a BIG THANK YOU!

My netball commitments were conflicting with my flying schedule and I had a choice to make which was easy. Netball came second.

There is a military lineage in my family. Whilst I was serving in the Women's Royal Air Force, my second eldest brother Cecil was serving in the United States Air Force across the 'pond' with his wife, Linda. He started his career as an English/Biology teacher at Mico Teacher's Training College, Jamaica but saw that the USAF recruitment figures were low due to the Vietnam War and joined in 1975. His first base was Little Rock AFB. He took a degree in Microbiology and posted to Andrews Air Force Base, Maryland where he could bring up his family in a stable environment. He embarked on two tours at Andrews; one tour at Bolling AFB; one at the Pentagon and two single overseas tours in Seoul, South Korea in twenty seven years of service.

My niece Yvette has proudly followed in her father's footsteps after taking a USAF scholarship in English at Princeton and her second a Juris Doctor's Degree at Georgetown Law Centre, both are Ivy League Schools. Unfortunately, Yvette has been medically retired as a Major. She was an Assistant Judge Advocate who assisted in court-martials and prosecuted Federal misdemeanours as a Special Assistant United States Attorney.

She is married to Roger Bourcicot, a Harvard history graduate. Their swish wedding was featured in the Washington Post September 2008. My nephew, Everton, named after a famous English Premier football team did not wish to follow his parents or sister into the USAF. Instead, he took his degree in Actuary at Temple. His first choice was Pennsylvania University.

Both my brother and sister-in law are USAF decorated veterans. There is a history of relatives on both sides of my parents who represented the Army in Jamaica and in Britain post WW2. Sadly the younger generation on the British side of the Atlantic do not hold a military interest.

Linda was given 'pole position' on the day of President Obama's inauguration 2009 to view his swearing–in as she now works for the Federal Emergency Management Agency (FEMA). The building is aligned to the west side of the Capitol steps.

Passing-out Parade at RAF Hereford December 1978

Val's RAF Log Book

SECTION 3

Year 1987 Month	Date	AIRCRAFT Type and Mk.	No.	Pilot	Aircrew Duty	Flight Details	Day (1)	Night (2)	TOTAL Captain (3)	Spare (4)
—	—	—	—	—	Totals brought forward		591.50	422.55	1014.45	
JAN	12	VC10 MK I	XV107	FLT LT SMITH	AIR STEWARD	BRIZE NORTON – Gardermoen	1:00	:45		
JAN	12	VC10 MK I	XV107	FLT LT SMITH	AIR STEWARD	GARDERMOEN – BRIZE NORTON		1:35		
JAN	15	VC10 MK I	XV102	FLT. LT D'DONOVAN	AIR STEWARD	BRIZE NORTON – GARDERMOEN	1:50			
JAN	15	VC10 MK I	XV103	FLT. LT D'DONOVAN	AIR STEWARD	GARDERMOEN – BRIZE NORTON	1:40			
JAN	19	VC10 MK I	XV103	SQN LDR WOOLEY	AIR STEWARD	BRIZE NORTON – BAHRAIN	7:00	1:10		
JAN	26	VC10 MK I	XV103	SQN LDR WOOLEY	AIR STEWARD	HONG KONG – JAHURUBU	3:35			
JAN	26	VC10 MK I	XV103	SQN LDR WOOLEY	AIR STEWARD	JAHURUBU – HONG KONG	3:05			
JAN	28	VC10 MK I	XV103	SQN LDR WOOLEY	AIR STEWARD	HONG KONG – BRUNEI	2:35			
JAN	28	VC10 MK I	XV103	SQN LDR WOOLEY	AIR STEWARD	BRUNEI – HONG KONG	2:30			
JAN	31	VC10 MK I	XV103	SQN LDR WOOLEY	AIR STEWARD	HONG KONG – COLOMBO	5:50			
JAN	31	VC10 MK I	XV103	SQN LDR WOOLEY	AIR STEWARD	COLOMBO – BAHRAIN	5:00			
				SUMMARY FOR January	AIRCRAFT TYPE	MONTHLY TOTALS	34:05	[illegible]	36:35	
				DATE 3rd February	VC10 MKI					
				UNIT TO SQN.						
				SIGNATURE [signature]		PROGRESSIVE VC10 TOTALS	257:05	77:20	334:25	
					Totals carried forward		625:55	425:25	1051:20	

Operational flights logged for January 1987

N I C

WRAF Basic Training November 1978

ROYAL AIR FORC
951

A portrait of 216 Tristar Squadron

Posing with colleagues in green flying suits for a war role

Karnival Club, RAF Bruggen, November 1981

French paratroopers

Trista 500 crew on the tarmac in the Ascension Islands

A NBC warfare suit

WRAF Brize Norton netball team

The Maersk refuellers, Ascension Island

Typhoon Prototype, Farnborough Air Show, July 2002

Landed back at Dulles International Airport after an exhausted and gruelling three-day shuttle to Belize

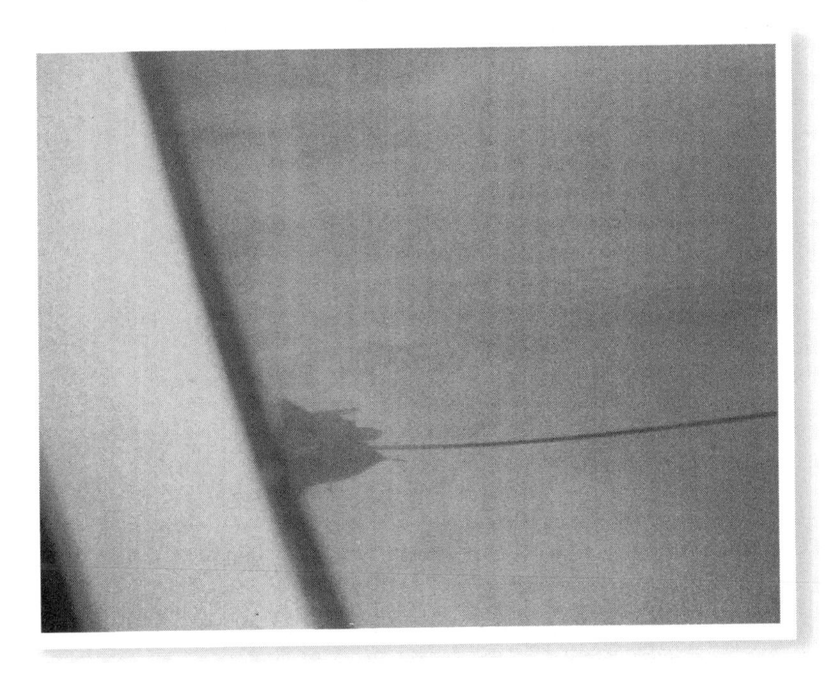

Tornado pulled up to VC tanker for air-air refuelling

WRAF Germany skiing championship and Snow Survival course held at Oberammageau and Garmisch

A Christening party at RAF Brize Norton 1983

CHAPTER FOUR

1980 – 1990

My next base was RAF Bruggen, West Germany. In January 1981 I arrived as the camp brought its war exercise to a close. Bruggen was the number one base for operational activities and this was a pivotal time when relations between the east and west of Europe were entente instead of detente until President Mikhail Gorbachov announced glasnost (openness) and perestroika (restructuring the economy) in one of his famous speeches.

The first information I received at Bruggen was that a police dog handler was awaiting his court martial for bestiality! I was given a shared dormitory with Heidi who was a Kennel maid. The Dutch Royal Air Force had given the base an Alsatian dog as a mascot in a gesture of goodwill. This dog grew and grew until I became frightened of its size. Whilst preparing myself a bath in the bathroom which was off the main corridor, I had returned to my room for some bath gel. On my return to the bathroom I saw this dog bounding towards me with its playful eyes staring at me. I managed to reach the bathroom and frantically locked myself inside gasping for air. The well bred dog was subsequently trained as a future police dog.

Six months later I returned to my room after work and noticed a stranger sat on the spare bed in the dormitory. I introduced myself to her and she replied who she was and why she was posted to the camp. She informed me that she was originally from RAF Gutersloh and was awaiting a court martial with her two friends (one was posted to RAF Rhinedahlen and the other remained at RAF Gutersloh) for being caught in an 'uncompromising act'. The WRAF Station Standing Orders No. 6, states that two or more females in a bedroom must have 'both sets of feet firmly planted on the ground and the door open'. The Homosexual and Lesbian Act was not passed for a further fifteen years.

The camp was built on a swamp and when it rained it left large puddles of water by the trees. In the summer months the wooded areas were swarming with thunder flies and mosquitoes. Barbeques were held on a Sunday accompanied by apple schnappes, Asbach brandy, etc with music blaring out to Motown and 80's Pop. It was English soil implanted into German soil until I went through the main gates and socialised with the local community.

On the 11th of November at the eleventh hour (Armistice Day) the German Carnival commenced its festivities. The festival ran until the beginning of March with clubs from neighbouring cities visiting each other on a Saturday evening once a month and revelling in um pah pah music and salutations to ein prosit!

The typical Bruggen women's outfit was a scarlet red cotton bolero jacket with white laced trimmings, a matching Nelson style hat with a white feather on the right side and white patent leather mid-calf boots. The men wore a bottle green Robin Hood hat with a brown feather sticking out on the left, beige shirts, short bottle green Lederhosen with tapestry braces, brown knee length socks tied with red ribbons and plain black/ brown leather laced up shoes.

When it was Bruggen's turn to hold the Carnival night the main aircraft hangar was used for this purpose and could hold up to a thousand people. I was an honorary member of the club and decided with the WRAF that we would put on a show for the camp. With the help of the Physical Education Instructor we choreographed a dance to 'The Sound of Music'. I was petrified of making a fool of myself but with a little encouragement from an apple schnapps I overcame my nerves. I pretended to be the youngest sister singing 'So Long, Farewell'.

The hangar was kitted out with wooden tables and benches, carnival buntings hanging across the stage, windows and walls. Pitchers of beer were sold at a relatively cheap price, alternatively asbach brandy, schnapps and vodka were also available for ein prosit salutations. The evening went down as one of the best evenings spent at the base by military personnel.

The Munich Beer Festival is a must. Twenty years later I was shown the area where members of the Manchester United Football Team (Busby's Babes) perished in the BEA Elizabethan airliner after it stopped to refuel at Munich Airport and had two aborted takeoffs and on the third disaster struck.

The city of Monchengladbach, 'with its street of a thousand pubs', in all its colour and gaiety swelters in the heat and humidity. On a Friday evening the soul club in the city would attract all black serving personnel from all the German bases. I remember vividly walking into the airmen's mess at RAF Bruggen and seeing a black arm protruding from a divider beckoning me. I was curious to know who this 'arm' belonged to and was introduced to Glen. He, in-turn, introduced me to the 'soul brothers' that were in his company. He told me months later that if I had ignored him he would never have spoken to me again!

In the midst of all these hectic activities, I forgot my 21st Birthday until I checked my mailbox and had received a dozen cards!

There was no let up on the many things to see and do. The Frankfurt air show attracted military and commercial aircraft manufacturers to display their latest prototype in operation. The Rhine-in-Flames boat trip was also a spectacular annual fete not to be missed. The boat journeys to the middle of the Rhine Valley with the biggest firework display taking place in Koblenz.

The European town and cities of Osnabruck, Bielefeldt, Cologne, Dortmund, Hamburg, Sennalager, Munster, Tryol and Maastricht are all beautiful places to visit each with its name linked in history. The historical city of Hanover is linked to King George I who was born there and became ruler of England during the 17th century.

Attached to the camp was the American unit called 'Big-Ear', the equivalent to the Government Communications Head Quarters(GCHQ) who listened in to the activities of the time. The Quick-Response-Action of the fighter jets, Jaguars and Tornadoes, were located near the RAFG golf course which the wild boars had dug up and ruined. The fighters took off at a steep incline leaving a trail of debris and dust behind. The QRA site was off limits to serving personnel apart from those who worked there. My boss, Warrant Officer Warren obtained permission from the local authority to kill these boars and serve them as table d'hôte for dinner one Saturday evening in the officer's mess!

During the Christmas festivities the Rumtopf Jar (traditional Christmas pudding) was served as the dessert. Many years later I was a guest at the Army and Navy club opposite St James's Palace which reminded me of the grand opulence of these impressive buildings and their wares. The ornate door handles, high ceilings carved and etched in gold, portraits of members of the Royal Family and distinguished former members of the Armed Services. The bay windows that looked out onto the manicured garden and courtyard and the historical rugs that protocol states one does not walk over.

The Fighter Pilot Series was aired during the summer of 1981 and featured a streamlined fighter pilot who was a single male who made all the commissioned and non-commissioned females feverish below the collar with his Cliff Montgomery looks. This pilot was streamlined to become an air ranking officer. I remember very vividly when a fighter pilot did not return from a sortie, a barrel in the officer's mess was laid on in his memory. (Female fighter pilots were not recognised in the RAF for another ten years).

Years later I visited the Farnborough Air show and received an adrenalin rush when the Euro fighter (Typhoon) prototype taxied, came to a standstill with its afterburner burning with fuel in preparation for take-off. Take-off and landing are the crucial phases of a flight.

The planned scenario war exercises lasted for four days and nights and unplanned war exercises up to four hours duration. An unplanned exercise caught men and women in relationships jumping out of windows and running back to their accommodation with one shoe missing, scarcely dressed when they heard the wailing of the siren. The scenario was 'real' until nuclear fallout and this was an indication for the 'all clear'.

The station was either on black or red alert – an imminent attack or attack. The atmosphere was tense, there were 'fatal casualties and minor patients' who were ferried to the medical unit with the van sirens flashing. The patients were marked with a Y or N depending on the extent of their injuries.

July 1981 saw conflict between the youth and police in the

district of Moss Side. I had just arrived from Germany on leave, Janet and I were walking round the local brewery when someone approached us and asked us the way to Moss Side? I did not think anything else about his question. Janet and I continued walking and talking when two black police vans sped pass us with their sirens blaring. The following evening I turned on the television to see a riot had broken out in Moss Side. Shops, including a well renowned boys and gents, were set ablaze because the youths were tired of high unemployment, dilapidated housing filled with asbestos and poor prospects of education in the throes of a mini recession. They felt the local council and the government were not listening to their plight.

It took another fifteen to twenty years (the Common Wealth Games) and funding from the European Union for the city to be given a face lift. Deluxe apartments and part-ownership and Housing Association properties sprouted up and have made a stark difference.

In June 1982 Prince Phillip visited Bruggen. The station leapt into sporadic action. It was an all male occasion except for the staff who waited on the guests for each and every whim. He came to view the operation of the Jaguar Squadrons of 14, 20, 31 and 25 Bloodhounds Squadron which was later decommissioned.

The camp was situated 10 minutes in no-man's land from the Dutch border town of Roermond which had seen skirmishes with the South Malaccans who were fighting for independence from Holland. If you travelled 50 minutes north east you entered another Dutch city called Venlo. Venlo was great for shopping and food. Wegburg, Rhinedahlen, Wildenwratth, Laarbruch and Bruggen were known as the west 'clutch-area' and Gatow, Gutersloh were the east 'clutch-area'. These were areas that came under British control after Germany was divided up by Britain, America and Russia post WWII.

On a skiing trip to Oberamagau where the Passion Play is held every 10 years I travelled on the military train which sped along the *train corridor*. The military train carried two days ration in the hold in case the train broke down. At each station from Hamm to Oberamagau the guards came on to check our permits and papers and trade souvenirs with us. When I started flying in the RAF I took a picture from the cabin of the approach into Tegfel/Berlinn along the *air corridor*, with its rolling hills and verdants. The aircraft would bank but could not veer off course as this could spell trouble as this was a hostile time between the western North Atlantic Treaty Organisation (NATO) and the eastern Council for Mutual Economic Assistance in Europe (COMECON).

Oh how things are so different since the collapse of the Berlin Wall. I remember the amount of red tape bureaucracy was created to travel from West to East Germany through Checkpoint Charlie. Cities such as Innsbruck, Funchal, Gibraltar and Hong Kong (Kai Tak the old airport) require specialist flight crews for the approach between big jagged boulders to land on these islands.

Skiing in Oberammagau, Garmisch and the Zugfelt in Innsbruck brought out my snow survival skills especially during the WRAFG snow-ski championship of 1982. (In later years when I transported the Army on ski exercises to the arctic circle on the VC10 aircraft which carried a Type 'A' Pack containing muklucks, parkas, crampons and icepicks, I felt prepared in case these items were required).

As a competitive sportswoman who represented the station at netball and WRAFG badminton, I also participated in cessna flying over Duisburg, gliding over Bruggen's air space and water-skiing in Skofel. Indulgence flights and excursions were heavily subsidised by the Air Force which was great!

September of 1982 I went on a fact finding trip to Tunisia to seek out her rural customs and traditions which included a three-day trip to Tozeur, Zur and the Djerba oasis in the Sahara Desert riding on a dromedary camel. The temperature rose to a staggering 120 degrees Fahrenheit. I took on extra water every five minutes as I was very dehydrated from the sun. I was fifty miles from the Algerian border and I decided to seek a cool shade in the form of my Bedouin tent. I travelled to Hammamet after a day's recovery and visited the capital Tunis where the old Kings and Queens are buried in catacombs.

I returned to my base in Germany from which I would soon leave for the UK. I had a great tour and did not want it to end but in order to pursue my goals it was time to leave. I was given the choice of catching a flight from RAF Wildenwrath and tackling the underground with all my kit or catching a Hercules flight from camp and landing at RAF Lyneham, scheduled for closure as part of the defence cuts to cope with the nation's debt crisis. Near the base is also the celebrated town of Wootton Bassett, given the royal seal for the innovative and seminal role it played in the repatriation of military bodies from the Iraq and Afghanistan conflicts.

I chose RAF Lyneham. I was then picked up by military transport and driven to RAF Brize Norton which was one hour and fifteen minutes journey time. The city of Oxford is situated 30 minutes from base; home of the country's most renowned seat of learning. The old shops with their cobbled pavements and mock Tudor look framework watching over the Thames with its passengers punting along the river.

September 1983 saw the USAF Detachment of the B52's

arrive at Brize Norton instead of RAF Fairford as their runway had split. I was given a private tour in the belly of the B52 with some comrades and also a trip to USAF Lakenheath. Another highlight of 1983 was seeing Air Force One.

My overseas tour had given me a major setback in my pursuit for cabin crew as the ruling had changed whilst serving overseas. Overseas assessments were not regarded when applying for the position as cabin crew. How bitterly disappointed I was that I would wait a further two years for my opportunity to fulfil my dream! In the meantime I knuckled down to achieve two years excellent assessments, had my interview in August 1984 and commenced my VC10 course November 1984. In the meantime I had another royal visit to prepare for, the Princess Royal, Princess Anne in October.

The RAF placed an order by the Air Ministry with the aircraft manufacturers Vickers in 1960 for five VC 10's, for 10 Squadron. British Overseas Airways Corporation (now British Airways) in May 1981 delivered 14 super VC10 MK1 abbreviated C1 to the RAF and one to RAF Duxford Museum. Special features for the military aircraft included Conway MK 31 engines with thrust reversers on the outboard only, an auxiliary power unit (APU) in the tailcone to supply ground electrical power, a re-inforced cargo floor, 137 aft facing seats(146 high density), a large cargo door and provision for in-flight re-fuelling. The VC 10 Tanker, 101 Squadron was fitted with a nose in-flight re-fuelling probe and close circuit television (CCTV) for a hose basket to connect with. It seems in modern day warfare the USAF prefers to refuel from the VC10 Tanker.

The VC10's are named after Victoria Cross (VC) medal holders, displaying the VC holder's name above the forward passenger door. In 1982 the VC10 were part of the *airbridge* operation between Brize Norton and Wideawake airfield, Ascension Island to retake the Falkland Islands.

I felt the world was my oyster as I was about to fulfil my dream and embark on my flying career. The flying programme consisted of a two-week ground school phase followed by a further four weeks training in emergency drills, emergency equipment, first aid, standard operating procedures, survival and rescue, security, in flight catering, passenger handling, aircraft technical, wet dinghy drills including aircraft visits (one of these visits had the aircraft configured in the VIP role for the Queen on a night leg fitted with a Divan).

I went on a decompression chamber visit to RAF Loughborough, the Tropical and Aviation Medicine centre where I was taken off oxygen for a minute and a half to experience the useful time of consciousness. As part of the exercise, instructions were given to write my x3 table after coming off oxygen for 90 seconds. I found that I had scribbled like I had done at the age of four!

My visit to RAF Mountbatten, Plymouth for my wet dinghy drill saw me shudder at the choppiness of the sea the night before I was to experience being ditched at sea. The seahorse waves remained the same on the Friday morning when four Army detachment soldiers were instructed to right the MS10 Dinghy with me. I was given the role of the sea survivor who was to be duly rescued by 'Johnny Weismuller'. My don suit leaked! As part of the sea exercise I waited up to 2½ hours in the dinghy for a Wessex helicopter, (that has since been decommissioned), to winch me up to safety. I sat in the bath for two hours just to allow the hot water to permeate my skin as the first signs of hypothermia were quite clearly visible.

It was six weeks of intensive training including two

familiarisation flights and one flight assessment. I was certified to fly and awarded my brevet and logbook. (Flight crews and loadmasters who had reached 10,000 flying hours would put on a barrel on a Friday evening to celebrate this feat; I attended a handful of these events during my tour).

Flight time limitations protect and govern a flight or cabin crew member on how many hours he or she can work per sector depending on the time that shift commenced. For every square inch on a map of the world is the equivalent of two hours flying time and equates to time bands and zones to acclimatise to down route. My very first flight was to RAF Akrotiri, Cyprus. On the outbound journey I had an army passenger who seemed very ill and pale. I went to attend to him and realised he was intoxicated and therefore did not require oxygen but some water or black coffee. The rest of the outbound leg went smoothly but the inbound sector to RAF Brize Norton was fraught with hungry and wet babies, severe turbulence due to torrential rain and fog that was creeping in. The aircraft diverted to RAF Marham, Norfolk. After landing the captain was informed that the station had just completed a war exercise, it took nearly two hours for some steps to arrive at the aircraft. The steps that were brought were engineer steps that the crew used to disembark the families onboard. When I fell into bed I had been on my feet for 16 hours! This was my very first flight in aviation and it has always stuck in my mind.

During my second tour on the VC 10 I flew several times with a Canadian Captain who was on an exchange detachment from the Canadian Air Force. The USAF bases that I flew to were split with commercial bases such as Tacoma/Washington (home of the Boeing manufacturers)or Dulles/Washington D.C. There were crews who felt I had a pad in D.C. as I was always rostered on the three to nine days stopovers because my brother lived in the triangular region between D.C., Virginia and Maryland.

Nellis Air Force base, located thirty minutes from the Las Vegas strip in the state of Nevada, annually held the red (friendly) and green (foe) flag exercises of which I was a proud participant. The VC 10 Tanker assisted in refuelling the fighter jets from all NATO countries who participated in aerial dog fights to show off their flying prowess over the Nevada desert which is the size of the states of Rhode Island, Connecticut and Wisconsin combined. The one memorable breathtaking scene is of the Mirage, Tornado, Gripen and Draken flying through the piercing blue sky and scudding clouds vertically upright, banking left/right and hovering like a vulture over its carcass.

I have had the opportunity to attend on the 8th December The Day of Infamy commemoration in Pearl Harbour, Hawaii when President F.D. Roosevelt urged the American people never to forget the attack by the Japanese and to memorialise the date in history.

The Calgary Stampede is a rodeo exhibition that bills itself as "The Greatest Outdoor Show on Earth". My flying operation in the Air Force would take me to nearly all the continent and to some exotic hotpots in the world.

Families Day at Brize Norton involved everyone from the cleaner to the Station Commander and civilians in the neighbourhood. The day's programme was advertised three months prior to the date of the event. Volunteers were required for charity events and fundraising and many were recruited from off duty personnel from the Fire and Police Sections, Medical Staff, Catering Squadron and Mechanical Transport.

Oxford Chamber of Commerce provided the base with local

wares and the Supply Squadron supplied the stalls with outdoor materials, buntings and electrical appliances. The aircraft hangar dispersed the VC 10's and Tri Stars to the airfield for fixed wing display and visits to the aircrafts. Human Resources, Catering Squadron, Tactical Communication Wing and No.19 RAF Regiment Squadron flung open their doors to visitors from London, Swindon, Oxford and the local town of Carterton.

Carterton was a shanty town previously occupied by the USAF post WW2 and transferred to the RAF in 1976 with its married quarters. The Cotswold is a region on the outskirts of Oxford. It is a valley of escarpments where the vast land tilts and richly attracts the retired wealthy. It lies between the counties of Oxfordshire and Gloucestershire. There was a crowd of 500 watching a fine aerial display of the Harrier (now decommissioned) hovering over the runway bulbs and shattering it to shards of glass. The RAF band playing RAF signature tunes. Later on in the evening there was celebrity entertainment from Alvin Stardust singing "my cuck–oo-achoo" in the aircraft hangar. With fine weather, excellent music, good food and drinks flowing from the bars set up in the hangar the event was a success.

A few professional highlights of my flying career in the Air Force was the Inauguration flight to RAF Mount Pleasant airfield, Falklands with Mr. Heseltine the Defence Secretary including British Airways Pursers who were seconded to the Tri star 216 Squadron. Celebrity participants of the South Atlantic Entertainment Crew were Harry Secombe and Jacques Cousteau Sr. who gave up their time to entertain the troops. On my second tour of the VC 10 I had the privilege of serving a high ranking Rabbi, Air ranking officers in the Air Force and senior executives from the Ministry of Defence.

The downside of the Atlantic run occurred when I carried a passenger travelling to Brize Norton who had received a "Dear John letter" and had fallen asleep with the letter encased in vomit stuck to his chest! The seamen who worked in the south Atlantic could be away from their loved ones for up to a year and this could be very distressing for their loved ones back home.

The Maersk and the Esk were Danish contract refuellers stationed in Ascension Islands who refuelled the Tri Star 500 and the VC10. The crew would meet up with the lads for some downtime after duty with sundowners watching the sunset in St Helena.

From Ascension to Brize Norton I carried a sick premature baby in an incubator with a team of medical staff who monitored Poppy's health during the flight. After the aircraft landed back at base there was another medical crew positioned to take care of baby for the journey to the John Radcliffe Hospital, Oxford. The good news was Poppy made a fine recovery.

During the summer months in Ascension there wasn't much to do but to sunbathe. My colleague Courtney would often say to me "get back in" my accommodation so she could catch up with my tan! A beautiful spot on the island was Bluff Cove. It was a truly a sight to behold with its turquoise lagoon, white sandy beach, the smell of salt water and the warm sea breeze encapsulated my consciousness. I woke up at one o'clock in the morning to go down to the beach with a colleague to search for turtles laying their eggs during season. Anyone caught disturbing turtles could be fined up to £250.

On a sector from Falkland Islands to Ascension Islands I carried 250 Penguin eggs mainly King pens but also Emperors; unfortunately two eggs cracked before landing. Scientists from the UK wanted to do extensive tests on these eggs. There was always a minimum of 15 knot wind all year round on the Falkland Islands and one evening during Burns Night myself and the crew went in search of penguins at Ben's Cove. We had walked for an hour and a half and dusk was falling with no penguins in sight. The temperature had dropped and the wind had picked up. The loadmaster, Jerry expostulated that whenever he found these penguins he would kick some butt!

On a delayed leg from the Falkland Islands to the Ascension Island my crew were informed that the inbound aircraft had diverted to Ascunscion, Paruguay. The story that was divulged out of the delay was that of a British passenger who was inebriated and used his shoe to knock on the British Embassy door. This could have caused great ramifications for the British government as this incident occurred during the Junta period in South America, but it passed without a murmur.

The crew were invited to HMS Proctor in the south Atlantic for a few drinks with the all male crew onboard. One of the lads was celebrating his birthday and thought it was a brilliant idea to blow up neutral coloured condoms as party balloons!

A visit to HMS Odin was another memorable trip, exploring the rudiments of a torpedo submarine that has since been scrapped. A 10 day expedition to the Falkland Islands, Antarctic Peninsula and Whale watching could set you back £2,000.

From Ascension Islands to Brize Norton a sergeant who had spent six months on tour was given the responsibility of demonstrating the lifejacket to the rest of the transit passengers. We were given special dispensation by the Civil Aviation Authority. The poor guy was inebriated and failed to demonstrate the lifejacket successfully and was offloaded. He had to spend another month on the island as his punishment for being drunk on duty.

A Chinook crashed on the Falkland Islands in July 1985, I was part of the crew that cas-e-vac (casualty evacuation) the Chinook crew to Brize Norton, the cabin was 50% configured for an aero-med role. There were two crew members with broken arms, one with a broken leg and two were on swivel stretchers with multiple neck and back injuries.

On a day-to-day basis I could fly in one of five roles which were: all passenger load, passengers with freight, passengers with dangerous air cargo, full–freight and aero-med. Full freight meant a reduction in a crew complement for the flight, the cargo would be lashed down with a special strap to keep it in place for the duration of the flight.

I would be briefed separately for a VIP flight or war role including air to air refuelling which called for me to wear my green flying suit. I remember refuelling a fighter over the North sea on a sunny clear day. The pilot of the Tornado came up on the right side of the VC10 Tanker where the fuel is stored under the wing, he took three attempts for the hose basket to connect to his fighter. The rule of THUMB is that a commercial aircraft must fly at least 1,000 feet apart from another aircraft.

In November 1985 it was the war widow's and veterans 40th anniversary of WWII which was named Operation Clarendon. I was involved in the first leg from Brize Norton to Bahrain. Apparently I was featured on the defunct ITN one o'clock, six o'clock and 10 o'clock News demonstrating the safety equipment. Unfortunately a colleague swiped it on her VHS tape unwittingly.

The crews for the second and third sectors had flown overnight to Bahrain and Singapore to be in position when the aircraft arrived at their destinations. The pilgrimage was hailed as a phenomenal success across the military. These celebrations have continued over the passing of the years. Operation Clarendon was regarded as a high profile flight but I also covered low profile flights for example to Brunei which is a British Protectorate transporting Army personnel for Jungle exercises.

The Tumbledown Tour commenced at the site where the 40 Marines were sprung a surprise attack by the Argentines. A poignant moment came when I covered the area where the Welsh Fusiliers fell during the capture of the islands and were temporary buried there. They have since been exhumed and interred in North and South Wales. In September of 1985 I was informed that my flight from the Falkland Islands to London Heathrow would transport a 20 year old fireman that I vaguely knew. He was a funny, articulate and intelligent lad who was racing his colleague in his jeep at full speed on a treacherous part of the road on the island when it toppled over and killed him instantly. We arrived at Heathrow at peak time and the captain was instructed to go into a HOLDING PATTERN. This is where the aircraft goes around until Air Traffic gives the captain permission to land. I am sure this was distressing for the parents who were waiting to receive their son's body as it was another 50 minutes before we could land.

I was also involved in the repatriation of the Duchess of Windsor, Wallis Simpson from Paris, Charles De Gaulle to RAF Brize Norton in July 1987. The presence of a member of the Royal household and dignitaries meeting her body meant that she would still be given royal status even in death.

During the Barcelona Olympic Games of 1992 I reported to Newcastle airport for an evening return flight to Rhodes. The captain briefed the crew that we would carry a deceased passenger on the inbound sector. The deceased and his wife were on honeymoon with two close friends when he collapsed and died at a bar after drinking his twenty-fifth tequila! The wife was escorted to the plane by the ground staff and her two friends who comforted her throughout the flight. The lady was three months pregnant at the time and could only be half sedated for the journey home. I was given the appropriate paperwork for the deceased cargo by the ground staff which I duly handed over to customs as I did on previous occasions.

I felt my second tour with the VC 10,10 Squadron was extremely challenging and demanding; the sectors were 14 to 16 hours especially to Calgary, Canada or to Hong Kong via Colombo, Sri Lanka. In Calgary the crew would eat at a well loved Japanese restaurant. The staff there would prepare and serve a delicious meal in front of you.

I was always suffering from jetlag on these punishing sectors and did not hesitate to fall asleep over my meal helped by a Saki night cap! On the Cannonball Run (20 hour stopover) to Washington DC I picked up a four hour delay when I reported for duty. The crew returned to their residents and I took Jenny, a married crew member to the WRAF block where we had a kip on makeshift settees in the living room. We still had to conduct our flight to Washington DC.

After checking in at the Holiday Inn Fairfax, Virginia Jenny and I decided to go shopping. Derek, a crew member from another flight whom we met in the lobby said he would come too. Jenny and I decided to have a nap and woke up two hours later in our adjoining hotel rooms bleary eyed and wondering where we were! When I woke up I felt my room was like a ship being tossed on the high sea waves. I tried to get on my feet but fell back awkwardly on my bed as I had no strength in my legs to hoist my frame upright. I was extremely exhausted.

Back at the base, I was taking part in tea in the airmen's mess with eight extraordinary service personnel when the meal was interrupted by a call that one of the lads had received from their commanding officer to say they were recalled for an assignment to the Mediterranean. In the services quick reaction is always required and what one trains for is used on a daily basis or in a specific case.

In December of 1986 the celebrity cartoonist Bill came to Brize Norton to gain some feedback from the VC10 crews for an airline cartoon that he was working on. I wasn't feeling well and put this down to fatigue but what really occurred was that I had naively cut out all sugary intakes resulting in a drop in my sugar level and this caused me some numbness and tingling in my hands and feet. I went to my doctor on base who referred me to RAF Wroughton for further analysis where my blood and urine samples were tested. These tests proved negative.

I was sent to the King Edward VII Hospital in Midhurst, Surrey for a Magnetic Resonance Imaging (MRI) scan. They administered iodine which did not show up anything on toward and left the medical staff perplexed with no answers. I spent three weeks worrying over the Christmas and the New Year period pondering whether my flying career had come to an abrupt end. In the early part of January 1987 I travelled to the Command Medical Establishment on Goodge Street, London to be certified to fly again. I sighed deeply with enormous relief.

British Airways Cabin Crew Course July 1999

Receiving my brevy from the Cabin Crew Manager

Fwd vestibule of a French Concorde

Inter-European Airways uniform

Valerie Wood

CABIN CREW

Cardiff-based British Regional Airlines cabin crew member Valerie Wood joined the company in the summer of 1999, but she is no stranger to the world of aviation, nor to the travel industry in general. Valerie, who for a while worked in public relations with cruise lines including Royal Caribbean and Cunard, has returned to her first love — airlines — after four years as part of the Servisair ground handling team at Manchester Airport.

She now lives just outside Cardiff Airport and is delighted to be back working with passengers, especially on the new Embraer jet, her eighth aircraft. "I've always loved travel" she says, "and specially enjoy meeting the passengers, many of whom have become familar faces on some of our routes out of Cardiff."

Valerie actually served in the Royal Air Force for nine years, flying on Tristars and VC10s and as cabin crew serving many high-ranking RAF personnel. She was stationed at RAF Brize Norton for a while, and lived in Germany for two years.

Not surprisingly, given her breadth of experience of so many aircraft, she says that one day she would like to learn to fly, and she also harbours a desire to write a book.

Off-duty, Valerie enjoys playing volleyball, netball and badminton. As far as holidays are concerned, she now says: "I've seen so much of the world in the course of my career, that these days I really like staying pretty close to home." With more time, perhaps, to start work on that first novel?

Posing in the new British Airways uniform, September 2005

Giving a pep talk to pupils at Manor Primary School, Newham

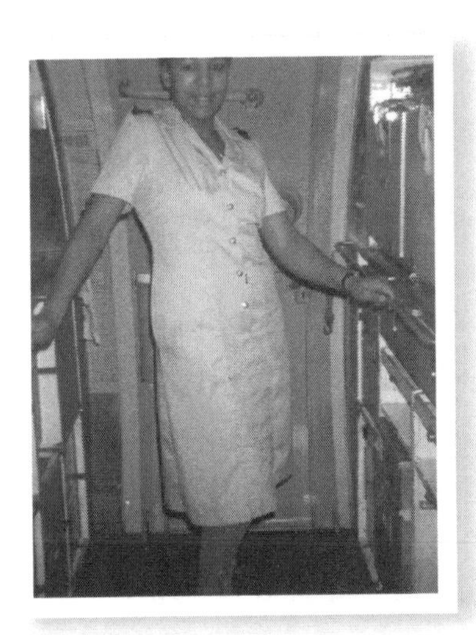

Galley of a VC10

Stood at a Satellite gate at Manchester Airport

Posing on top deck of the QE2 with New York Harbor in the backdrop

With friends on board Royal Caribbean Cruise Lines

CHAPTER FIVE

1990 – 2000

Although I was relieved to resume flying, I was now anxiously preparing for civilian life in the real world instead of the cosseted and pampered establishment I was familiar with. My commanding Officer of the VC10 Squadron wrote a glowing report on my discharge papers. He said: "Since joining the Royal Air Force in 1978 Corporal Wood has been employed in Officers Messes as a Steward. In 1985 she was selected for training as an Air Stewardess and was trained for these duties on VC10 aircraft, the primary passenger aircraft in use in the Royal Air Force. After only a short period on the VC10, she was posted to Tri Stars where she obtained a Senior Stewardess post. She returned to duties on the VC10 for her last year of service where she worked to an above average standard. Corporal Wood is a keen sportswoman playing netball and badminton at representative level. She has stated her intention to apply for a cabin crew post with a civil airline for which her buoyant personality and cheerful disposition are eminently suited".

I joined Inter European Airways (now Thomas Cook) in the spring of 1988 as a Senior Cabin Crew Member operating the Boeing B737/300/400, B757/200 and Airbus A320 to Europe, the Mediterranean including the Greek islands and the Middle East. At the beginning of the First Gulf War in 1991 the company took the names of all ex-military members who were on the reserve list, myself included, who could be called up at any stage. I still had eighteen months left on the reserve list.

There were Flight crews who were ex-Navy pilots, ex-Army helicopter pilot and former RAF Hercules pilots. As part of the company's operation if I was required in Glasgow or Edinburgh they would fly me in a chartered air-taxi, a Cessna in order to connect me with an onward flight. This was a regular occurrence during my contract but heard in the media years later that a similar flight carrying (My Travel) crew had crashed with loss of life and some serious injuries.

On a night stop in Amman, Jordan I went on a religious excursion to Mount Nebo (Mount Pisgah) where Moses viewed the Promise Land. It was spell bounding as I am a person of faith. Later that same year I travelled to Tel Aviv, Israel during Hanukkah and visited Manger Square which is a special time in the calendar. The Western Wall notes that are left in the cracks by tourists are now digitalised – this has come with the breakthrough in technology.

I received a spiritual uplift when I visited the river Ganges; the river Goddess, Ganga, who cleanses the ashes of the dead and is revered by Hindus. The peace and tranquillity of the river Ganges and its tributaries were clearly evident.

Hindus have a ritual bath below the temple as a sign of crossing over from earth to heaven. The river is shrouded in myth and mysticism with the backdrop of the Himalayas and its supernatural powers. The carps that are one metre long and weigh 50lbs swimming down river to spawn, the mountain monkeys jumping limb to limb in the Tree of the Gods, the red star and porkdale birds all give zest and a colourful life to the Ganges.

There were a few Cardiff crew members who felt I was conceited as they misunderstood my very high 'standards'. A crew member later told me that they had misjudged me as a person. In the bible it states "only a foolish man/woman is wise in his/her own conceit".

Manchester, my home city, was the company's main hub for flying. The crews based there were recruited from different airlines and had a broader perspective on aviation and appreciated my work ethic and high standards. Janet, my sister who is a social worker, could be very vitriolic concerning my high standards. Our brother, Cecil has intervened and given Janet the elementary lessons in high standards in the Services. I will always feel proud to have served this nation in the Women's Royal Air Force.

My next career goal was to bring some semblance of balance in a different method of transport and decided to join Royal Caribbean Cruise Line (RCCL) in the spring of 1993. Initially, I joined the 'Sovereign of the Seas' which was the flag ship for RCCL. Upon completion of my training I was transferred to 'Song of America'. All the original ships were sold and replaced by 'Ocean of the Seas, Legend of the Seas, Splendour of the Seas', etc. I spent the summers of '93 to '95 based in New York at 7th Avenue and cruising between New York and Bermuda. I have had the opportunities to fly to Bermuda with the RAF and cruised with RCCL. I was fearful with trepidation if I would be caught up in the mystery of the vortex called the Bermuda Triangle.

During the winter months based in San Juan or Miami we island hopped to the colourful, vibrant and steel band playing islands of St. Croix, St. Kitts, Nevis, Guadeloupe, Martinique (home of Empress Josephine), Trinidad & Tobago (home of Carnival), Antigua, Anguilla, St. Maarten, St. Thomas, St John, Tortola, Bahamas, Jamaica, Barbados (Cropover Festival), Dominica and Labadie.

The diversity of the staff on the ship was astronomical with

51 different nationalities all having to respect and recognise each other's differing needs and value the perspectives that each bring from their culture. I am always keen to develop an atmosphere of openness and trust. I also endeavour to show courtesy and respect to all individuals irrespective of their hierarchy or heritage. I found that a few of the Central Americans lads from Costa Rica, Nicaragua and Honduras were indifferent to me as they felt I was looked on more favourably because I was British.

I enjoyed spending quality time talking with the lads form the ship and at the local bars on these islands catching up on some patois or visiting a famous cricket legend's house. It was a great opportunity for me when I watched the England Cricket Team play one of their tests in Antigua in 1994.

The Trinidad Carnival is a colourful sight to behold – a sea of variegated faces and costumes in synchronisation with the splendour of the music; the beat of the steel pans bellowing out and the whistles being blown intermittently.

As I joined the Cruise Ship, 'Song of America', I was told the story by the ship's photographers of a card game that went horribly wrong and became violent as one man thought the other had cheated and wound up with him being knifed to death. The survivor was a staff member who had recently transferred to another RCCL ship, 'The Viking'. This incident occurred in Norwegian waters so it was dealt with by the port authorities who handed the guy to the police where he was placed in custody in Stavanger. When his case came to court he was handed a prison sentence of fifteen years in jail. His wife and children emigrated from Jamaica to be nearer to him. He completed an engineering degree and they are all living happily ever after in Norway!

My cruise contract lasted three to four months, 78 hours per week without a day off until I took leave for a mandatory two months vacation. I would spend my first two weeks on leave with my head barely leaving the pillow! I would feel sluggish and drank energy drinks to give me a boost. It also meant that my immune system was tried and tested when I fell ill with an asthma attack shortly after arriving home after my first contract was completed.

On an eerie approach into Martinique the sea patrol captain came aboard and took command of the 'Song of America' and manoeuvred the ship into harbour as per usual in November 1994. All the Swedish and Danish bridge officers had congregated on the deck as was custom except the Swedish Captain. The Captain's deputy sent a staff member to the captain's room to ascertain why he was not present on the bridge and found that he was dead! The ship's doctor was summoned and pronounced him dead from a heart attack. The ship was delayed in port for eight hours whilst special dispensation was dispatched from immigration and customs to place the body in a walk-in freezer on board until the ship arrived in Trinidad where the captain's body could be flown back to Sweden. This was a distressing time not only for the officer but for all the ship's staff as he was a friendly and polite man.

Marking another arrival into Trinidad, a Jamaican steward was kidnapped by some local lads as he descended down the gangway of the ship. There were rumours that he owed these lads some money! Apparently he managed to escape from his kidnappers and possessed sufficient money on him to fly back to Jamaica. His belongings were taken off the ship by security personnel when we returned to base in San Juan, Puerto Rico.

Thinking back to earlier that year, the ship was docked in

New York harbour and I was waiting to disembark. I noticed a Vincentian guy nervously twitching and pacing back and forth. It is a ten minute walk from the ship through the hangar to the hot musty smell that greets me as I hit 88th Street. Unbeknown to me the port authorities had been tipped off to apprehend this guy. He managed to resist arrest and fled from the hangar before the police could catch him. I spotted him the following week waiting on the other side of 88th Street for a colleague who had some of his effects as he was still being pursued by the police.

On some leisure time in St. Kitts I and two colleagues went to our favourite meeting place 'Hole in the Wall', a family bar managed by Noel, a Jamaican man and his Kittian wife Martha. We arrived at 2pm. I kept my eye on the time as the ship was due to set sail at 4pm. I noticed that the time was quickly slipping away. At 3:15pm I mentioned to my colleagues that we should be heading back to the ship as time was of the essence as they were on Black People's Time. They wanted to stay a little longer as we could view the ship from where we were sitting. I began to feel uneasy and there was some tension in my voice. They tried to reassure me but it was in vain. It is now 3:45pm when we set off for the ten minute drive in the café owner's car. As we reached the ship the on-duty security man started pulling up the gang plank! We managed to get his attention and he lowered it again to let us on. I vowed after that near miss I would always give myself sufficient time to return to the ship.

The passengers and I would converse in great lengths about the meals on board and the daily activities. A veranda café breakfast consisting of Danish pastries and tea/coffee would kick off the day about 6:30am, followed by 1st or 2nd sitting English breakfast or Brunch. Lunch between 12noon to 3:30pm. Later on in the afternoon, ice carvings and ice cream. A lunch pack was provided if an excursion was booked. Afternoon tea consisting of open sandwiches and clotted cream, jam and scones around 16:30 – 17:30. French, Italian, Dutch or German dinner was served depending on the theme for the evening and finally supper with a country and western or Caribbean theme.

As a Seventh Day Adventist, attending church means a great deal to me. I was elated when the opportunities arose in places such as Belfast, Dusseldorf, Nassau, Port of Spain, New York, Nairobi, Johannesburg and Cape Town. I met some of the nicest people on board RCCL; one couple left me a note stating to follow my dreams whether it be air, land or sea. Just be happy! My dear friend Cessine from New Jersey each year sends me a Birthday, Easter and Christmas cards since 1993.

I decided to have a break from cruising and joined a Swedish free-lance firm Air Ops and flew short and long haul sectors. The crews were mainly Swedish with a sprinkle of British. The crew members that I interacted with were fascinated with my cultural background as Sweden, at that time, was not as diverse as it is today. I particularly found the trips to Lourdes and the Hajj rewarding, as they carried the sick and needy who required some spiritual inspiration and divine intervention.

The Queen Elizabeth II liner lured me back to cruising and I spent one contract cruising as part of the world itinerary in July 1995. The guests were the high end of travel – 'repeated' passengers who just loved the North Cape – the breathtaking scenery of the Fjords, cliff hanging glaciers and the Northern Lights (Aurora Borealis with its bands of white and green lights). The Land of the Midnight Sun where the sun does not set and where the months between October to February has hardly any light. The Ice Palace in Tromso which starts to thaw mid-April. The Tall Ship Race from Edinburgh, the stunning ships with their graceful line bedecked with colourful bunting.

Coronation Street actors who were promoting their books boarded the QE2 as guest speaker passengers when the infamous 38 feet waves occurred! During the hurricane season (September to November) the ship could be tossed like a toy on the choppy sea. I would have that gut wrenching feeling when the ship would embark on a spell of bad passage. The length of the QE2 with the carriage of 1800 passengers meant the ship had to dock at the Naval Dockyard and bus the passengers into Hamilton, Bermuda whilst the 'Song of America', a 52 tonnes ship that was previously owned by RCCL carried 1500 passengers and could moor opposite the High Street in Hamilton. The QE2 is now moored in Dubai as a 5-star floating hotel.

The time had arrived for seeking a fresh challenge, a new project. It came with the National Vocational Qualification (NVQ). I was a pioneer for the NVQ's in 1996. I became a recruiter and Assessor in Travel, Customer Service and Business Administration. The job took me all over the UK promoting this new and vibrant qualification. My targets were based on the winning of contracts and these soon started to dry up as the market became saturated with different agencies bidding for contracts. I decided to bow out.

I took up a similar aspect of travel on the ground at Manchester and then Cardiff Airport as a Passenger Service Agent. Responsibilities included check-in, passenger handling, baggage enquiries and air bridge operations. I enjoyed working on the ground checking-in the Rugby Airlift passengers from Scotland, Ireland, Wales, England, France and Italy which formed the Six Nations Tournament. It was unique but not unusual to check–in pet owners and their pets for a flight. On a Manchester to Glasgow flight a Gun party bought a ticket for the Gundog to travel in the cabin but only Dogs for the Blind and Deaf are permitted to travel in the cabin.

I soon felt restless in my sleep and considered returning to flying for British Airways. I joined the airline operating regional flights from Cardiff as a Purser. I flew on the Inaugural flight for the Embraer 145. A local editor Stephen Ritch wrote, "Valerie Wood joined the company in the summer of 1999 but she is no stranger to the world of aviation nor to the travel industry in general. Valerie, who for a while worked in public relations with cruise lines including Royal Caribbean and Cunard, has returned to her first love – airlines – after four years as part of the Servis Air ground handling team at Manchester airport.

She now lives just outside Cardiff Airport and is delighted to be back working with passengers, especially on the new Embraer jet, her eighth aircraft.

"I've always loved travel" she says and specially enjoy "meeting the passengers, many of whom have become familiar faces on some of our routes out of Cardiff".

Valerie actually served in the Royal Air Force for nine years, flying on Tri Stars and VC10's and as cabin crew serving many high-ranking RAF personnel. She was stationed at RAF Brize Norton for a while and lived in Germany two years.

Not surprisingly, given her breadth of experience of so many aircraft, she says that one day she would like to learn to fly and she also harbours a desire to write a book.

Off-duty, Valerie enjoys playing volleyball, netball and badminton. As far as holidays are concerned, she now says: "I've seen so much of the world in the course of my career that these days I really like staying pretty close to home". With more time, perhaps, to start work on that first novel?

Months later I reached a special landmark, my fortieth birthday and spent it in Manchester with family and friends throwing a celebratory party.

British Pullman Orient Express, No. 5 carriage, Perseus, pulled the body of Sir Winston Churchill at his funeral

Taking a cruise down the Danube with a close friend, June 2004

Mount Nebo (Pisgah) where Moses viewed the Promised Land

Miami Boardwalk with RCCCL ship in the background

Overlooking Diamond Head, Honolulu, Hawaii

Outside the Motown Studio, Detroit

Awards of some of the Motown stars

In Red Square with a Moscovite conscript

"Storming the Winter Palace", St Petersburg

Raffles Hotel billiard board where the infamous tiger was shot

Kuala Lumpur sentry guard and me

Porter and Doorman in the lobby of the Safari Club Hotel, Nairobi

Nairobi Seventh Day Adventist Church

Cape Town Seventh Day Adventist Church

Cape Point where the Atlantic and the Indian Oceans meeta

Inside Nelson Mandela's cell with Eugene, a fellow prisoner and now guide (Eugene No 23-83, 1983-1990)

The spot where Mahatma Gandi was assassinated. His house is nearby

Porter and Doorman inside the Imperial Hotel, Delhi

In front of the majestic Taj Mahal

Midway of the River Ganges

My Shanghai hotel

Doormen of my Shanghai hotel

On a Safari

Safari driver and Safari friends

Sunn City, South Africa

Rift Valley Triangle of Kenya, Uganda and Tanzania

Sam Lord's Castle, St Philip, Barbados

Vasco Da Gama football stadium,
Rio De Janeiro, Brazil

Stood by the Welsh Fusiliers' burial spot at Tumbledown, Falkland Islands

Sydney Opera House, Australia

CHAPTER SIX

2000 – (PRESENT)

I returned to my home city on a relocation package and continued to operate regional flights out of Manchester including to New York on the B767/300. This flight was always full to capacity. Some interesting passengers were the older Osmond brothers and Jewish families travelling during the Purim Festivities. I found their conversations fascinating as I am a Seventh Day Adventist and our religious beliefs are very similar. The city that 'never sleeps' with its Manhattan skyline always sprung a surprise, especially when I met family friends that I have not met for thirty two years on Christmas Eve 2004! That evening I had reserved a seat to see George Balanchine's 50th Anniversary of *The Nutcracker* performed by the New York Ballet Company.

On an inbound flight from New York to Manchester the crew were waiting in the lobby of the hotel on 44th Street East for the arrival of the outbound crew transport to take us to JFK airport. Transport arrived on schedule and we all boarded on schedule. An inbound crew member was informed by an outbound crew member that the aircraft had an aileron problem. This information was not passed onto the captain. We arrived at JFK and were greeted by the Duty Manager who whisked away the Captain, First Officer and Cabin Service Director. The rest of the crew were asked to proceed to the Terrace Lounge to await further information. Within thirty minutes news had filtered through that indeed the aircraft had an aileron problem which is a hinged flap on the aircraft wing. The aircraft was now a no-go which meant it was grounded. It was decided by operations that the crew would position back on the next available flight. The crew members who had checked-in their luggage went to retrieve them from the baggage drop off area. The rest of the crew that had hand baggage only commenced stuffing ourselves silly on a variety of snacks that were provided by the lounge staff. Forty five minutes later the rest of the cabin crew greeted us with elation because they were checked–in to First class seats! The Cabin Service Director who was in my company promptly proceeded to the Terrace check-in area and we too were given 1st class seats. It remains my only experience travelling in First class. It felt special. I cast my mind back to early 2001 when a BA flight bound for New York had a technical problem, the passengers were all rebooked on the next available flight bar one passenger who decided to show his allegiance and wait 24 hours for the aircraft to be fixed. He was pictured next to the prepared aircraft for a full flight including the hold containers, First Class catering, Club Class catering, Economy catering and all the staff required to put the flight together.

In March 2007 British Airways pulled its operation out of Manchester Airport. This action affected the flight crews, cabin crews, dispatchers and customer services staff. The morale plummeted to an all time low as we all felt like one big happy family that was being broken up. Depending on one's contract one would be re-interviewed for their jobs or transfer to a new role under TUPE (Transfer under Present Employment) arrangements and relocated.

Business does not remain the same in aviation. If you are in possession of a laptop you can commute from A to B and so in April 2007 I started commuting to London City Airport. The airport is very unique as it is categorised as an executive airfield with a very short runway. You can check-in and board a flight to New York within fifteen minutes! During the two week shutdown in the summer holidays whilst the business scheduled flights are quiet, the charter flights are extremely busy. I was asked by the London City Airport Community Relations Department if I would represent the company in my capacity as cabin crew for Black History Month 2008. I gave Manor Primary School pupils in the borough of Newham a pep talk in my current role as a Purser, from reporting for a flight, preparing the cabin (cleanliness and checking safety equipment), meeting and greeting the passengers and take-off. It was both refreshing and rewarding that the pupils were very knowledgeable in aviation and some would like to become pilots and cabin crew when they grow up.

Whilst I was on a standby duty at LCY airport, November 2008, the airport evacuation alarm went off. The BA standby crew were asked to assist in the general welfare of the other airline crews and passengers in the car park. A table was set up in the grounds of the car park where the staff canteen replenished hot water urns, tea, coffee and biscuits that we offered to everyone. Two and a half hours later a smouldering cigarette was found in the ladies toilet bin. The standby crew were all given new duties which meant I would be heading home very late to Manchester.

January 2010 I was briefed for a routine flight from LCY to EDI that I would be carrying the former Prime Minster the Right Honourable Gordon Brown accompanied by his wife and children. After I gave the crew their mandatory brief and prepared the cabin for departure, the BA Station Manager and co-ordinator started counting down – 45 minutes for the PM's arrival to LCY airport, at – 15 minutes the PM arrived on schedule with his entourage. He and his family were greeted, seated and the aircraft took-off at the estimated time of departure.

Janet has always reminded me that I am always in a hurry in my career and in life in general. I have had an illustrious career and had face to face experiences with some high profile people (including a four legged Red Setter that won Crufts in 1992) but have remained humbled throughout my experiences, whether it came from the Women's Royal Air Force, members of the Royal Family including a visit to Blenheim Palace in the presence of Prince Michael of Kent, French Concorde, QE2, Royal Yacht Britannia, the British Pullman Orient Express, The Taj Mahal and the Hippo Lodge – Kenyan/Tanzanian border safari. Robben Island, the isolated place where Nelson Mandela was incarcerated for 27 years. Lenin's glass tomb, situated in Red Square (his nails are manicured every year because of the embalming). Hitsville USA/Motown where some great artists made their first hits such as Stevie Wonder, the O'Jays, Diana Ross and Marvin Gaye.

I have had the good fortune of operating and positioning as crew and passenger on twenty one aircraft types and seven variants.

The story of Solomon Grundy comes to mind and the nursery rhyme that 'Thursday's child has far to go'.

Multiculturalism can work but I would need to quote John Lowery who walked with Martin Luther King during the civil rights movement. At the end of President Obama's inauguration benediction he said: "when black will not be asked to get back, when brown can stick around, when yellow will be mellow, when the red man can get ahead, and when white will embrace what is right".

In the years ahead of retirement I hope that the Royal Chelsea Hospital will open their doors to ex-WRAF personnel as I and other ex-RAF members see it is a comfortable place to retire with its manicured grass and pristine buildings. The hospital is steeped in history as it was King Charles II who financially provided his wounded Army personnel with its facilities.